* STYLE IT: TRENDS AND FADS

Makeup Magic

by VIRGINIA LOH-HAGAN

45TH PARALLEL PRESS

Published in the United States of America by
Cherry Lake Publishing Group
Ann Arbor, Michigan
www.cherrylakepublishing.com

Reading Adviser: Beth Walker Gambro, MS, Ed., Reading Consultant, Yorkville, IL
Book Designer: Joseph Hatch

Photo Credits: Jhong Pascua/Pexels.com, cover; © Gao-feng/Shutterstock, 4; Zeyneb
Alishova/Shutterstock, 7; Image courtesy of Cheekbone Beauty, 8; Mo-kao Caves, Public
domain, via Wikimedia Commons, 11; National Portrait Gallery, Public domain, via
Wikimedia Commons, 13; © Kathy Hutchins/Shutterstock, 14; Public Domain, New York
World-Telegram and the Sun Newspaper Photograph Collection, Prints and Photographs
Collection, Library of Congress, 16; Artem Podrez/Pexels.com, 19; Konstantin
Mishchenko/Pexels.com, 21; Ebenezer Idowu/Pexels.com, 22; Ron Lach/Pexels.com, 24;
© Kiselev Andrey Valerevich/Shutterstock, 27; © lielos_photograph/Shutterstock, 28;
© Sang Cheng/Shutterstock, 31

Copyright © 2026 by Cherry Lake Publishing Group

All rights reserved. No part of this book may be reproduced or utilized in any form
or by any means without written permission from the publisher.

45th Parallel Press is an imprint of Cherry Lake Publishing Group.

Library of Congress Cataloging-in-Publication Data has been filed and is available
at catalog.loc.gov

Cherry Lake Publishing Group would like to acknowledge the work of the Partnership
for 21st Century Learning, a Network of Battelle for Kids. Please visit Battelle for Kids
online for more information.

Note from publisher: Websites change regularly, and their future contents are outside
of our control. Supervise children when conducting any recommended online searches
for extended learning opportunities.

Printed in the United States of America

Dr. Virginia Loh-Hagan is an author and educator. She is currently the Executive
Director for Asian American Native Hawaiian Pacific Islander Affairs at San Diego
State University and the Co-Executive Director of The Asian American Education
Project. She lives in San Diego with her very tall husband and very naughty dogs.

TABLE of CONTENTS

INTRODUCTION 5

CHAPTER 1: **Goat Hair Eyebrows** 9

CHAPTER 2: **Forehead Decorations**........10

CHAPTER 3: **Face Whitening** 12

CHAPTER 4: **Teeth Blackening** 15

CHAPTER 5: **Red Lipstick** 17

CHAPTER 6: **Glam Makeup** 18

CHAPTER 7: **Glitter Lids** 20

CHAPTER 8: **Dark Lip Liner** 23

CHAPTER 9: **Glass Skin**........................... 25

CHAPTER 10: **Faux Freckles**................... 26

DO YOUR PART! 29

GLOSSARY.............................. 32

LEARN MORE 32

INDEX................................. 32

There are always new makeup trends!
Which ones have you seen lately?

INTRODUCTION

Everybody has style. Some people have more style than others. They stand out. They use **fashion** to express themselves. Fashion is about how people want to look. It's about how people dress. It includes clothes, shoes, hats, and jewelry. It also includes hairstyles and makeup.

Fashion changes across cultures. It changes over time. There are many fashion **trends**. Trends are fads. They're patterns of change. They reflect what's popular at a certain time. Many people copy popular looks. They copy famous people. They get inspired. They want to be cool. They want to be in style.

Some trends last a long time. Other trends are short. All trends make history.

Your face is the first thing people notice. Some people use **cosmetics** to enhance their look. Cosmetics include makeup. They also include perfume, skin cream, and nail polish.

Makeup adds beauty to one's face. It includes lipstick, eyeliner, blush, and more. Makeup can also cover up flaws. It includes powders and creams.

Makeup can change how people look. It adds personality. It signals one's role in society. It plays a key role in fashion.

Some makeup is bold. Some is simple. There have been a lot of makeup trends. This book features some of the fun ones!

Makeup is used on actors. It can help them get into character.

FASHION-FORWARD PIONEER

Cheekbone Beauty was founded by Jenn Harper. It's one of the first Indigenous-owned cosmetics companies. Harper is **Ojibwe** and Canadian. Ojibwe are Indigenous people. They're from the Great Lakes area. Harper said, "I dreamt of Native little girls dancing, laughing, and just displaying such genuine joy all while covered in lip gloss." This dream inspired her to start her company. She did this in 2016. Her company represents Indigenous people. It's built on Indigenous wisdom. It supports eco-friendly practices. It protects the environment. It gives back to the Indigenous community. Harper said her products are "safe for both people and planet."

CHAPTER

One

Goat Hair Eyebrows

Ancient Greeks and Romans loved a thick **unibrow**. This is when both eyebrows meet in the middle. They're connected. Unibrows look like one long eyebrow. In the ancient world, they were mainly worn by unmarried women. They were a sign of beauty. They were a sign of wisdom.

Some women couldn't grow unibrows. So they made fake ones. They got goat hair. They dyed it black. They added it to their brows. They applied it with tree **resin**. Resin is a thick, sticky substance produced by some trees and plants in response to injury. It can be used as glue.

Women also used **kohl**. Kohl is black powder. Women used kohl to draw in eyebrows.

CHAPTER TWO

Forehead Decorations

Huadian is a traditional Chinese makeup style. It was popular from 618 to 907. Chinese women decorated their foreheads. But some also decorated their cheeks, temples, and dimples. Legend says the emperor's daughter kicked off this trend.

Designs were made with paint. These designs were mainly red. Green and yellow were also used. Designs included flowers, animals, and more. Plum blossoms were the most popular design. Other popular designs were birds and snakes.

Other items were added to enhance the design. These included paper, gems, and feathers. Fish scales and dragonfly wings were also added. Such designs signaled high class.

This fresco from the 900s was found in the Mogao Caves in China. These women have Huadian makeup.

CHAPTER

Face Whitening

Ancient Egyptians whitened the skin around their eyes. They wanted to look young. They wanted to look rich. Rich people didn't work outdoors. But the face creams they used had white **lead**. Lead is poisonous. It damaged the skin. It caused hair loss. It can cause death.

Queen Elizabeth I ruled England. She ruled from 1558 to 1603. She had **smallpox**. Smallpox is a sickness. It left scars on her face.

Elizabeth wanted to hide her scars. She wanted to appear to have fair skin. She used heavy white face paint. This paint also had white lead. Some experts think the face paint led to her death.

Queen Elizabeth I set many style trends.
Using white face paint was just one of them.

FASHION REBEL: TRENDSETTER

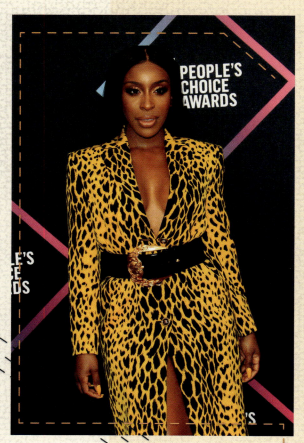

Jackie Aina is a beauty influencer. She makes YouTube videos. She started in 2009. She has millions of followers. She gives beauty tips. She reviews beauty products. She also promotes diversity. People listen to her. Companies listen to her. Aina's mother is Black American. Her father is Nigerian. Aina fights for Black people in the beauty business. When she shopped for makeup, people turned her away. She wanted to try new trends. She was told these trends wouldn't work for her skin color. This made her angry. She pushed for more makeup shades. She wanted makeup for darker skin tones. She worked with companies to make this happen.

Teeth Blackening

Queen Elizabeth I set another trend. She loved sugar. Only rich people could eat sugar. Elizabeth ate a lot of sugar. Her teeth rotted. They turned black. Women copied Elizabeth. They blackened their teeth. They used soot. They wanted to look rich, too.

Making teeth black was a beauty trend in Asia. People used pastes and dyes. Starting around 400, Vietnamese people blackened their teeth. They thought white teeth belonged to animals and evil spirits.

Starting around 800, Japanese people blackened their teeth. This signaled adulthood and status. Some Pacific Islanders also blackened their teeth.

This is Elizabeth Arden. In the 1920s, she was one of the wealthiest women in the world.

CHAPTER
five

Red Lipstick

Red lipstick has been around since ancient times. It's been a symbol of power. It's been a symbol of sin.

In the early 1900s, women were fighting for their rights. They were fighting for the right to vote. Elizabeth Arden built a cosmetics empire. She inspired women's rights leaders to wear red lipstick.

She gave out red lipstick to protesters. Red lipstick became a sign of rebellion. It was a sign of resistance. It was a sign of freedom. It was a sign of courage. It forced people to notice. Women were demanding change.

CHAPTER

SIX

Glam Makeup

The 1980s was a bold decade. People had big hair. Their makeup was big, too. Glam makeup is glamorous. It makes a statement. Popular color shades were bright, neon, and metallic.

The 1980s look included red cheeks and lips. People **draped**. This means they used large amounts of blush. They used bright pinks. Blush was applied beyond cheeks. It swept up to the sides.

The 1980s look included lots of eye makeup. People used thick blue eyeliners. They used long fake eyelashes. They used lots of eyeshadow.

Foundation is cream or powder. It's applied to the face. It covers flaws. It creates an even look. The 1980s look included layers of foundation. Foundation tended to be 2 skin tones lighter than the natural skin tone.

DIY FASHION FUN

MAKE YOUR OWN MAKEUP. MAKE YOUR MAKEUP LAST LONGER. HERE ARE SOME IDEAS:

» Make your own lip stain. Avoid smudging. Avoid fading. Apply your favorite lipstick. Leave it on for 10 minutes. Wipe it off with a wet cotton makeup round. Apply lip balm.

» Turn eyeliner pencil into gel. Hold the tip under a flame. Let it cool for 15 seconds. This makes eyeliners softer. This makes it easier to apply. Line your eyes.

» Have fun! Play with makeup. Try different colors. Try different designs. Do your friends' makeup. Maybe you'll even start a new trend!

CHAPTER seven

Glitter Lids

Glitter lids were also known as frosted eyeshadow. This trend added sparkle to eyes. It emerged in the 1990s and 2000s.

It was popular in Nollywood. Nollywood refers to the Nigerian film business. Nigeria is an African country. This trend was also made famous by U.S. pop stars. These stars included Britney Spears and Christina Aguilera.

Eyeshadow shades were shimmery, icy, or metallic. Colors were often silvers, whites, baby blues, soft purples, and soft pinks. People added these colors onto eyelids.

They also put these colors onto the corners of eyes. This created a frosted look. Frosted eyes look wide, bright, and glossy. This trend is still popular today.

Today, people are also frosting their eyelashes.

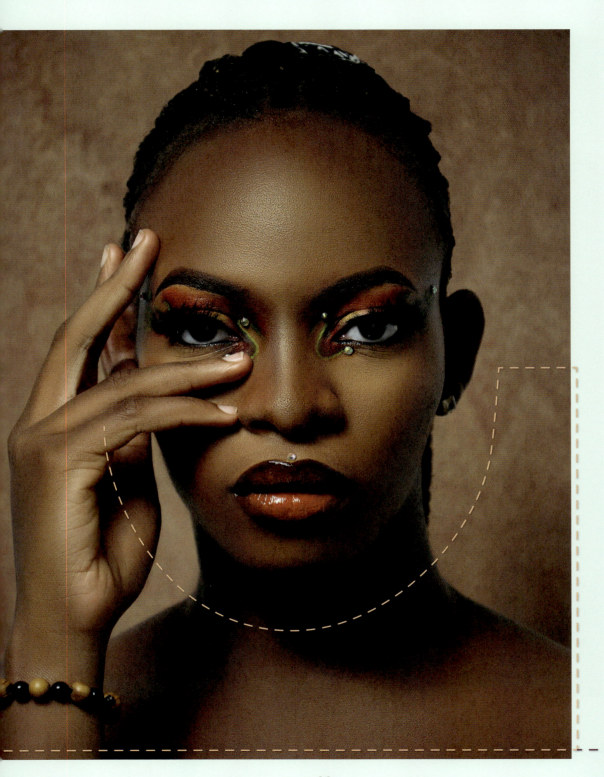

CHAPTER EIGHT

Dark Lip Liner

In the 1990s, a new lip trend emerged. It's still around. People contrasted colors. They used a dark lip liner. They used light lipstick colors. Before, people blended the colors. This new look was stark. The edges were bold. People wanted to see the 2 colors. They wanted to see the shape of lips.

Black women invented this trend. They didn't have lip liners that matched their skin tones. So they used brow and eyeliners. These liners were darker.

Some Latina women adopted this look. These women lived in Los Angeles. They were part of **Chicana** culture. Chicana women are people born in the United States. They have Mexican ancestors.

Adding some lip gloss completes the look!

Today, both men and women focus on skin care.

CHAPTER

nine

Glass Skin

Korean popular culture is a global craze. This includes Korean beauty trends. Since the 2010s, everyone wants glass skin. Glass skin is all about skin care. The goal is smooth, clear skin. Skin should look like glass. It should glow.

People clean their skin. They remove dead skin cells. They can use oil-based cleansers. This removes dirt and makeup. Then they can use a water-based cleanser. This leaves skin feeling clean.

People **hydrate**. Hydrate means to retain water. People can use face masks. They can use lotions.

People protect their skin. They use sunscreen.

CHAPTER

Ten

Faux Freckles

Faux means fake. Faux freckles are hot. They blew up in TikTok videos in the 2020s. Kayla Caputo is a fashion and beauty influencer. She said faux freckles gave a more natural look.

People make small dots. These dots are added around noses and cheeks. This gives a healthy, sun-kissed look. It covers flaws. It makes people look young.

People use liquid eyeliner pens. They use eyebrow pencils. Or they can use Freck's freckle pen. Remi Brixton is the owner of Freck Beauty. She wanted to "unlock the perfect freckle." She has always wanted freckles. She helped make freckles cool.

Metallic or glitter freckles are also popular.

When you go makeup shopping, try to buy makeup made without animals. Then have fun playing with it!

DO YOUR PART!

It's always fashionable to stand up for what's right. Fashion can be more than just about looks. It can be used to fight for causes. Be a fashion **activist**. Activists fight for change. They want a better world. Here are some ways to make a difference:

- Use **cruelty-free** makeup products. Many products are tested on animals. Cruelty-free means no animals were harmed. Protect animals.

- Use **vegan** makeup products. Vegan means no animals were used. Some products might contain beeswax or milk. Beeswax comes from bees. Milk comes from cows. Vegan products only use plants. They use vegetable oils and fruits.

- Buy **fair trade** products. Many beauty companies have factories overseas. Overseas labor is cheaper. This lets companies make more money. Fair trade means paying a fair price for labor. Protect human rights.

- Look for **sustainable** packaging. Sustainable means using resources carefully. Buy from companies that recycle. Buy less plastic. Buy makeup that can be refilled. Reduce waste. Save the planet.

- Respect cultures. Don't just copy cultural practices. Don't copy their looks. Don't copy their styles. Learn about people. Learn about their traditions.

Remember, every little bit counts. Kindness matters. You can look good and feel great!

FIGHTING FOR JUSTICE

The fox-eye trend became popular in the 2020s.

White people made it popular. They made videos. This trend makes eyes look slanted. This can be offensive to people with Asian heritage. Asian eyes are slanted. Some people have made fun of Asian Americans for their eye shapes. And now people are trying to copy them. They do this without learning about the history of anti-Asian hate. Many Asian American activists resist this trend. Jordan Santos is a Filipina American beauty influencer. She said, "The same look used by non-Asians to insult Asians for their eye shape is now being used for aesthetic purposes." Issa Okamoto is an Asian American social media influencer. She said, "My eyes are not your beauty trend."

Glossary

activist (AAK-tih-vist) person who fights for political or social change

Chicana (chih-KAH-nuh) woman or girl born in the United States who has Mexican ancestors

cosmetics (kahz-MEH-tiks) products applied to the body, especially the face, to improve appearance

cruelty-free (KROOL-tee-FREE) free from animal testing

draped (DRAYPT) applied large amounts of blush in bright pinks and deep plums to enhance cheekbones

fair trade (FAIR TRAYD) trade between companies in developed countries and producers in developing countries in which fair prices are paid

fashion (FAA-shuhn) any way of dressing that is favored or popular at any one time or place

faux (FOH) fake or made in imitation

foundation (fown-DAY-shuhn) makeup product applied to the face to create an even skin tone and cover flaws

Huadian (HWAH-TEE-yin) traditional Chinese makeup style

hydrate (HIE-drayt) add or retain moisture

kohl (KOHL) black powder used as eye makeup

lead (LED) a metallic element, poisonous with prolonged exposure

Ojibwe (oh-JIB-way) Indigenous peoples group around Lake Superior

resin (REH-zuhn) scented, sticky substance produced by some trees and plants in response to injury

smallpox (SMAWL-pahks) deadly disease that causes fever and scars

sustainable (suh-STAY-nuh-buhl) describing a resource that can last a long time without running out or harming the environment

trends (TRENDZ) fads or changes that are popular or common

unibrow (YOO-nuh-brow) when 2 eyebrows meet to form 1 long eyebrow

vegan (VEE-guhn) containing no animal products

Learn More

Anton, Carrie. *Skin & Nails Book: Care and Keeping Advice for Girls.* Middleton, WI: American Girl Publishing, 2018.

Eldridge, Lisa. *Face Paint: The Story of Makeup.* New York, NY: Abrams Image, 2015.

Rotta, Ikumi. *Makeup Is Not (Just) Magic: A Manga Guide to Cosmetics and Skin Care.* Los Angeles, CA: Seven Seas, 2020.

Index

Aina, Jackie, 14
ancient Egyptians, 12
ancient Greeks and Romans, 9
Arden, Elizabeth, 16–17

beauty influencers, 14, 16–17, 31
Black beauty culture, 14, 22–23
blush, 18
body art, 10–11, 26–27

Cheekbone Beauty (brand), 8
cosmetics, 6, 18
cosmetics companies, 8, 14
cruelty-free products, 29

dark lip liner, 22–23
DIY projects, 19

eco-friendly products, 8, 29–30
Elizabeth I, 12–13, 15
eyebrows, 9
eye makeup, 18–21, 23, 26, 31

face whitening, 12–13
fair trade products, 30
fox-eye trend, 31
frosted eyeshadow, 20–21

glam makeup, 18
glass skin, 24–25

Harper, Jenn, 8
Huadian makeup (China), 10–11

kohl, 9
Korean beauty culture, 24–25

Latina beauty culture, 23
lip liner, 22–23
lipstick, 17, 19, 23

Native-owned companies, 8

sustainability, 8, 29–30

teeth blackening, 15
theatrical makeup, 6–7

vegan products, 28–29